WINDOWS

OF

PERCEPTION

by

johnny solstice

Published by
Iliffe Independent
Leeds UK

ISBN 978-1-909110-144

www.iliffe.org.uk

wikilies.org.uk

A huge wad of money in my hipster pocket….lump like a rocket….
….inna nuther pocket….eight hundred and seventy2 orange
microdot..lsd….oh!…bugger me.. there appears to be ….approaching
me across the festival field of 19seventy2 or three….the worlds least
likely hippeee…. A cross between a flunky and a junkie…. Davy oota
the munkies crossed wi Blakey off the Buses…. There was no mistake
this was my wake…. Here was the Man… heading straight for me…
this was the 3rd degree…….No time to run and flee…
. PARANOIMALARM!….. PARANOIMALARM!…..
Swallathebloodylot
Swallathebloodylot

s…w…a…llow **theb**loody lot

lot LOT

LOT

Eight hundred and seventy two recurrrrrrrrrrrrrrrrrrrrrrrrrrriiiiiiiiiing

LOT**LOTTTT**s..mmmmmmmmmmmmmm…….lots

lost
found
unbound
dragged around

crash landed naked in a meadow in Wales….giggling with the
buttercups and butterflies…. When the smiley jacket people came to
collect me for some psychiatry they were perplexed to see how much
the buttercups and butterflies greived for me
and cried "come to tea….
anytime your free….

Don't be a stranger!
Don't be a stranger!…."
But stranger than this…….
was the kisssssssssssssss….
Of the farmysuitical rocKet
Head ripped oota its socket
Theres a prophet in every pocket

And my EIGHT- BALL is nailed to the wall

Wall

Wall

Wall

For walls that do dishes can have the crumbliest flakiest
family sized ...winamajurprize

sexShun Blah... of the HeADnoise Act 1953

Start collecting today wiv nuffink to pay...

...winamajurprize

Start collecting today wiv nuffink to pay...

Now its day.........

Now its night

Now its day.........

Now its night

Now its day.........

Now its night

Now its day.........

Now its night

Now its day.........

Now its night

Now what was that thing I mustn't 4GET?
KONKRETE SLIPPERS AND A MARZIPAN DRESSING GOWN
PLUS 5mg INTRAVIENOUS ARMCHAIR every hour.....
Drowning in the shower
KONKRETE SLIPPERS AND A MARZIPAN DRESSING GOWN
PLUS 5mg INTRAVIENOUS ARMCHAIR every hour.....
" Hold on john.....john hold on
Everythings gonna be all.......right

Sunlight cascading and tumbling the daffodil pollen of the dayroom
"mother…!
You had me….!
But I never had you…..!
Sunlight cascading and tumbling the daffodil pollen of the dayroom
Sunlight cascading and tumbling the daffodil pollen of the dayroom
Waddafugwozthatcon-con-con-kockshun they gave me this morning?
Somesomesomesome somekinda fugggggin speedball or summit?

HeADnoise

… of the

Blah… Act…….

NURSE RATCHET…..!
NURSE RATCHET…..! …..!
Eight hundred and seventy two recurrrrrrrrrrrrrrrrrrrrrrrrrrriiiiiiiiiing
FIVE hundred and seventy two recurrrrrrrrrrrrrrrrrrrrrrrrrrriiiiiiiiiiing
Two hundred and seventy two recurrrrrrrrrrrrrrrrrrrrrrrrrrriiiiiiiiiiing
19 quarters and seventy two recurrrrrrrrrrrrrrrrrrrrrrrrrrriiiiiiiiiiing
recurrrrrrrrrrrrrrrrrrrrrrrrrrriiiiiiiiiiing
rrrrrrrrrrrrrrrrrrrrrrrrrrriiiiiiiiiiing   rrrrrrrrrrrrrrrrrrrrrrrrrrriiiiiiiiiiing
rrrrrrrrrrrrrrrrrrrrrrrrrrriiiiiiiiiiing   rrrrrrrrrrrrrrrrrrrrrrrrrrriiiiiiiiiiing

"RING YOUR BELL IF YOU NEED ATTENTION"

NURSE RATCHET…..!
NURSE RATCHET…..! …..!
I WANT my cigarettes…
Billy's got Tourettes….
Jenny's got regrets…..about her figure
She got paranoid 'bout gittin bigger…
Self-harmed during her mocks
Gets messages frae the elektrik-shock
Jacob is washing my feet……….Telling me I am the chosen one

While a biblethumper talks in tongues….
says I'm to do whats never bin done
says the father is my son

"the Queen of the South shall rise up in the last days.......
                ....and win the Scottish Premier League.....
and the Antichrist shall walk upon the face of the Earth....
And he will avoid the Temples.... To concentrate his attention to
the ears

Meanwhile maggie kicksoff for a cuddle
Brian's in a bit offa muddle
And some meathead befuddled
With a helluva knuckle
Requires me for his Josephine tonight
"Just for tonight.!".."Just for tonight.!".."Just for tonight.!".."Just for tonight.!"
"Just for tonight.!".."Just for tonight.!".."Just for tonight.!".."Just for tonight.!"

so...........it takes six weeks of "Just for tonight.........!""
till they ascertain......
        that if not sane?
Then who's to blame?
Its just a game......
Its all the same.....
"And he's no next of kin...."
"Its almost a sin............. To keep this one in the bin...
                                .." said the Drake with a grin
"what time does the cabaret begin?" enquired a voice within

so they put me out to tender.......B+B.... hostel......rathole!
                        "stick it up your arsehole......."
And I'm off the rung again
There's a snake on every ladder
And things are getting madder

seventy two recurrrrrrrrrrrrrrrrrrrrrrrrrrrrrriiiiiiiiiiing
seventy two recurrrrrrrrrrrrrrrrrrrrrrrrrrrrrriiiiiiiiiiing

By the time the receptionist got round to mispronouncing my name it
was already mid-afternoon, so it was with some petulance that I slung
myself into the green-leather chair. I immediately got out the Mothers
Pride and proceeded to place a dollop of H.P. sauce on each slice prior
to folding and proffering them to the psychiatrist for his perusal.

"A conglomeration of amoral sound-bite sized wheaty delusions Mr Soltice" he proclaimed, after the sixth well-balanced slice lay before him in a sexually provocative manner.

"Let's try some sauce association, shall we?" he enquired reaching for my bottle.
"Malt vinegar?" he snapped.
"Jay-suss onna cross!" I blurted in response.
"Modified maize starch?" came the cross-court volley.
"erm…. Bovine spongiform encepolopathy?" I stuttered.
"Interesting….." he muttered whilst making hurried notes to my file which rendered it slightly out of tune.
"Tamarind extract?" he asked after a theatrical full-stop with his Parker pen.
My brain was now receiving no new incoming calls.
I was watching diplomas burning on his walls.
When a deep primeval voice rose from my balls.
"Haemaroid Hunchback..!" echoed around the room.

The psychiatrist fell backwards off his perch and landed on his cuttlefish, which gave him quite a shock.

"Haemaroid Hunchback..!"
"Haemaroid Hunchback..!"

"mister solstitz….really!" quacked the cycle-liar-twist, so I made good the escape by pulling down my roller-blind anti-ram eyelids and legged it along the woodland path between the pine-panelled diploma trees. After what seemed like an eternity masquerading as a nanosecond I tripped over a concrete Guiness can and began floating upwards till I banged my head on an overhanging branch of Woolworths, filled my nostrils with Pick n Mix and found myself lying in the foetal position surrounded by mistletoe-encrusted store-defectives.

"Wots your game then?" bellowed the one who was exactly the average weight of the other six.
"are you one of them inhalant assailants?" said another.
"oi bread boy… do …you…hear ….me?" (this may have been the first speaker or someone who sounded remarkably like him)

"Bag him and tag him and put him on display!" said a voice that
sounded like it was used to being obeyed.
Then the night turned into grey.
And the man at the pharmacy said:
"don't operate heavy machinery whilst you take this vow" "I Journey
Soul-Fits do swear by these Terms and Conditions…..
to swallow when you're told to
and never more to argue
to form an orderly queue
to jump when you'r told to
or we'll fry your grey matter
with molasses and batter
your head with a Runcible spoon"
Not a moment too soon
A fork in the room
Allowed me an exit of sorts
So grabbing a seat at the back of the bus
I ran through my spells with a baton.
"A swoosh shoe….!"
"A swoosh shoe….!"
"Bless you" said the cyclisp as I opened my eyes,
and to my surprise,
caught sight of his Freudian slip
all lacy and sexy
and quite fashion-risky
ejaculate onto my loaf
"Perhaps we should increase your dose?……. Mr Salt Ice can you hear
me? Do……you…….un…der…stand..?
We can never let you land
On our Holy Sinking Sand
Five milligrams of Seroxybland
Stuffed up you pucker gland
Should set things for a while
While we drain your brain for bile"
He then handed me a fresh bottle
So I pulled back the throttle
With just enough reserve to fight another day
And to the headless parrot on the wall
Who sees the fairest of us all

I tipped the wink and headed for the ball

twohundredandseventythird moon approximate

inna cornish cave inna state......
platform boots and cheesecloth shirt don't keep out no cold at
night.....but the days were red hot sunstroked peeling blisters
turning septic..... on the end of my nose hangs a bag of skin
butterbean sized and fulla pus..... head away along the shoreline
......rest between tides....day 5 the bag'o'pus explodes and a
little girl named Emily calls me a sagpuss and hands me a gift to
explain.....so I transmogrify into professor Yaffle....and find
myself inna chemist shop at half past 3am... rippingOut the DD
box....smelling like a fox..... in bad socks....

    Playing wi my mouse organ....
    Baited cheese for fire wardens....
    Keep ya in between the toxic borders...
    Mental health society disorder....
    Ye believers in sin make I grin
    Frae the inside of my loony bin
    Come ootside intae IN
    Come ootside intae IN

ART **BRUT**... ART **BRUT**

OUTSIDER....!

OUTLAW......!

OUTSIDER..........

outTHERE.....

SOMEWHERE
INBETWEEN
THE IRREGULAR AND THE DREAM

With my eyes wise open

The bible-thumper with nine bags of zeal
 With a toothy grin says his book can reveal
The one and only true definition of heal

But its pronounced con-ceal

"god is great…!"
"god is great…!" says Mr Fundulate

Hey Mr fun….fun…fun
Fun-da – mental
- mental
- mental-ism
           ism
         schism
what's your bloody ism?

CUBISM?   NUDISM?
SADISM?   MASOCHISM?
SADO-BLOODY-MASOCHISM?
CREATIONISM? SATANISM?
DUALISM?   PLURALISM?
CATHOLITHISM? CATHODE-RAYISM?
GONGORISM?
GONGORISM?
GONGORISM??????
(that's an affected literary styleeeeeeeeee…….!)
STIGMATISM?   DOGMATISM?
NEPOTISM?   DESPOTISM?
       ISOLATIONISM?
KON-KON-KONSUMERISM?

Yea…! Everyones got a little schism

"god is great…!"
"god is great…!"
might is right…!
Might is right..!
Majority rule
Majority rools
Demoktatik fools
Anarchy drools
at your GATE
GOD IS GREAT
GOD IS GREAT
Take me to your pearly gates
(*as soon as this bomb detonates…*)
    free me from the church and state
    (*oh..and those catholiks wot we hate*)

GOD IS GREAT
    GOD IS GREAT
        His books tell us whom we can hate
        TRIBALISM?   COLONIALISM?
            MATERIALISM?   IMPERIALISM?
            CAPITALISM?   FEUDALISM?
        COMMUNISM?   CONSUMERISM?
            CYNICISM?   NARCISSISM?
        SCEPTICISM?   MYSTICISM?
                SHAMA…..
                SHAMA…..
            SHAMANISM?
Vegetarianism……
Sacramentalism….
Nihilism… socialism
Vandalism
Sexism….. racism
What's your ISM?

God is great?
Holy shit..!
Would you adam'n'eve it?
Talking snakes.......
        and JOURNALISM

seventy two recurrrrrrrrrrrrrrrrrrrrrrrrrrrrriiiiiiiiiiing
seventy two recurrrrrrrrrrrrrrrrrrrrrrrrrrrrriiiiiiiiiiing

The smoke that swirled up from her pipe
hung there in the air, partly obscuring her
face

With cupped hands she began to gather the
Smoke as if it were sand on the beach

Very carefully she began stroking and teasing
it until it appeared to be taking on the
properties of a solid

What had been the contents of her lungs
Moments before, were now compressed to the
size of a tennis-ball

This blue-grey sphere hung there between us
like some strange smoke-filled soap-bubble

As I began to open my mouth to say something
a sword the size of a pin flew from my lips,
and burst the bubble whereupon the smoke fell
to the floor like fine white snow.......
            "...don't you know?"
        she said, with a grin,
    "...that's just the way that wars begin!"

As she refilled the pipe with twigs and weeds
she raised one eye-brow and a voice somewhere

between us said....."so you want to find
yourself, do you?........don't you know that
talking to yourself is the first sign of
'SANITY?"....

"And with that my mouth involuntarily said
"FORKS"
but the sound didn't come.....
                                instead
      from the side of her bed
came the unmistakable sound of forks falling on
a wooden floor......and everything began to
rhyme
        then I heard the chime
                of her quartz clock
            a rooster appeared,
          with an immense cock
          ....attached to it's head
                by the wind it is lead
          but East is opposite North instead

    then she scooped it up
      and it turned to twigs..
before my eyes could adjust....
......the phosphorous flash of IGNITION
                the firey INQUISITION
As she relit the pipe, with what seemed to be
                my thoughts and dreams made real
                    in solid words
                    in solid air
            I cried in deep despair
      for the weight of untold shame
                that showered like rain
          on those who could not explain
                      their own pain
            on those trapped in shame
            those crucified for vain
          making everyone to blame
                    for MY pain
              which falls like rain

                              into her upturned hand
                              where it forms a lake
                              called "my mistake"

Based on a lack or something missing
                         I can hear the hissing
                            of the black snake
                    the guardian of the gate
                    my birthright to legislate
                    catch fire before my eyes
                    as   another dreamy spire
                    of grey-blue smoke.......
                         ....rises into the void
for a brief moment the only rhyme is
                              PARANOID
              but just as quickly it is gone

As the pipe glows then rises musical notes pour
from its bowl as if the Mistral wind itself
were blowing through the embers.
Upon inhaling I am surprised to find that my
companion has been joined by Oscar Wilde...
heavily, theatrically disguised as an empty
chair
                    with accompanying wall-paper

This observation becomes solid in the air
and suddenly there are chairs everywhere
in my pockets, in my pipe, in my hair.....
chairs of every size and type and colour
everywhere…..no standing room, just chair upon
chair upon chair

"Collect your thoughts" said Oscar Wilde
to me, as if I was a naughty child

So, slowly, I gather the chairs together with
cupped hands, like sand, into one single chair

then lay my pipe upon it to make it real
from behind the canvas I step....my hands
reveal..

                    PAINT AND BRUSH
                       IN SUCH A RUSH
                    GRIND AND CRUSH
                       YELLOW OCHRE
                    CHROME YELLOW
                          yell "HELLO!"
                             "HELLO!"
                             "HELLO!"
....have you fallen in love with that pipe?"
asks the chair

                             As I stare...
             yellow sunflowers everywhere
festoon the walls, the floor, the chair……..
             elsewhere...
theres rubber clothes and x-ray hair
          starry nights and daymares
          loveless thighs and derrieres
          cut price love unguaranteed
   sure-fire ways to dispose of seed
right now...... with GREED-SPEED
          rivers of come, knee-deep
          bed's on fire.....can't sleep
 cut off my ears but they won't bleed
             instead they turn to weed
which I place on the chair with the pipe
and invite my companion to take her feed

   "...don't mind if I do" she replies
   "...but must we forever sit inside?"
   "..not far from here I think I spied"
   "... a cornfield......some countryside.."
"we could walk far, and near, and wide
 then round and left and right outside
 till darkness falls upon our heads.....
  and sends us scurrying for our beds"

But sleep won't come
because some elektronik hum
is buzzing in the walls
makes me shiver in my balls
till my spirit-level falls
and my skin begins to crawl
off my body,....up the walls
          reality DISSOLVES
.........skinned alive on a granite rock
......beneath the stars of future-shock
          alone.......
with billions of others
          with no cover
other ...than the cold blankets of mist
                              that hiss
        from the wounds in my wrist
                    reality persists
          CAN MY SOUL RESIST?
        WILL MY HEART DESIST?
  FROM BEATING IN MY BREAST
WILL MY BONES STAND THE TEST?
.......or will they crumble like the rest?
                    and be blessed
                          by her
        as she smokes me in her pipe ....
          I am scorched by her love
        that comes raining from above
                into my upturned hand
      and when I can no longer stand
              another day another night
              in this lifetime of fright
              and I want to take flight
          I drink her from my hand
  like fresh spring water on a summer's day
                    she makes my head sway
              to the natural rythm
              of her breath.......
              of her smoke.....
                  of her hair........
                  of her chair....

```
        of ANYWHERE
      where she is.....

She gives me back my skin
          fills me to her brim
then strikes another match
and draws me deep inside
  till I can no longer hide...
    my grin, a mile wide
I'm safe here inside
          .........outside
        .........inside
      THE VOID....
```

22 twenty two 22 twenty2 Recurring
22 twenty two 22 twenty2 Recurring

Victory V Speedy was jailed for persistently growing a beard
And sexually harassing a Nestles chocolate machine
When he got his custodial sentence
They called his de-fence
An o-ffence
And promptly gave him thirty
For daring to talk dirty
About the emperors shirty
And the Tom & Jerry
Nightly
Dose
Of cathode radiation
And presidential termination
In the land of the playstation

"objects in the mirror may appear closer than they are"
"objects in the mirror may appear closer than they are"
said Speedy from his celluloid pad
"I've a feeling I've been had…..
this is not so bad"
"The emperor must have had………….
…..a bloody big mirror"
"….god I wish I was thinner
and I'm strangely drawn to T.V. dinners"
(though I'm sure I'll never get a dress to fit)

"A Fishermans Friend is no substitute for Victory Vees
Your fuckin' mind's diseased"
said Speedy as he squeezed
his bony frame between the bars
and rode the shooting stars
as far to the east as he could lean
"have you ever been…..
…….B4?"
enquired a talking door

that opened in the floor
some thirty stories high above the ground

"I don't think………but maybe once upon a dream
my eyes have seen
a similar scheme
involving pyramids and green
…….frog skin
but they are not my kith or kin
with their holy savage sins
and their child-proof loony bins
they're but wholves in sheeps-kin

"Keep yur noize doon Sonny-Jim"
said the warden with a grin
"set yur pilot-light tae DIM
it's thyme fur the mane feetchur tae begin……."

"have you got any wildlife.....?"
asked the brash young reception officer
"....I'm sorry....?" said the outlaw, " ..I don't understand your question..."
"CRABS...LICE.....NITS.....COCKROACHES....LURGY....
.things living
in your crevices?" retorted the uniform,
"......oh!..I see what you mean
I thought this was a dream
and you wi' your tongue
was gonna lick my rung
and see for your fuckin' self.....?"
so they threw me in the block
naked on the rock

just below the water-line
where I perched for a while
till I learnt a swimming style
and swam the golden mile
straight back to my cell
and the pleasant hell
of the incarceration
of my vibration
yes I swam that mile
in the free-est of style
of a man without an shore
just rowing without an oar
till I got washed up
and they hosed me down
then became their clown
so they rung me out
and hung me out to dry
with all the old lagging
on a barbed-wire clothes line
and I got a piece of paper
saying "we'll see you later....
if you try another stunt like that..."
"....yea!..we'll see you later
in the playground
after skool

and we'll bring our diplomas
and our freudian rools
then we'll show you who's boss
as we nail you to the cross.....
a victim of your own
SUBLIME KRIME

22 twenty two 22 twenty2 Recurring

When your spirits ill at ease
your body produces a dis-ease
So you take your body to a vampire quack
who makes up a potion of mumbo-jumbo

call it ism and condria
cons you with his sigh-antifik
use of dumbo-mumblo-cashflo
HYPO-critikal
spurt-blood-surgikal
symptom removal.....
and the spirit cries out
"HEAL ME!......HEAL YOU!"
"HEAL ME!.....HEAL YOU!"
"HEAL ME!.....HEAL YOU!"
I'm me!.....so are you!
What are we gonna do?
You heal me and I'll heal you
Fix the 'isms with your mind
Heal your body don't be blind
Charge my battery, change your fuse
If I die what will you lose?

"they'll cut you hopen
wiv a carkin knive
then weigh your blotches
minus boils an'pus
meazure it an' pleazure it
an' when they canna figure it......
them stick it wi' a label called...

NATURAL CAUSES"
when your heart pauses
they get honey on their pawses
dipping into the jar
giving the patient a scar
to add to his collection
of silly-con injections
that maintains his erection
which under close inspection
is just another chemical reaction
from the pharmaceutical fractions
who give our spirits contractions

As our inner fires put out
by non-biological water-spout
gushing through our veins......
.........and organs
.....and ducts
the "keep 'em chilled" human "toilet duck"
gets into your brain (fucked)
PARA-PARA-PARALISED
with paranormal PARANOISE
X-RAY specs and polaroids
cash back on your haemorrhoids
makes the bankers jump for joy
and use you like a guinea toy

OI!
YEAH YOU!
PHARMACEUTICAL CREW
I'm talking to you.....
wot paints the sky blue
YEAH YOU!
top pharmaceutical crew
here's a lesson to you....

FUCK YOU!
THEY'RE COMING FOR YOU
'AINT NOTHING YOU CAN DO
the people see through...
your webs and your lies
your corporate flies
on the shit of humanity
your eggs-instant a.......
.......PROFANITY
Theres no limit to your depravity
you live as a cancer on the back of the cured
your patented medicine impure...
PUREES THE BRAIN
With dis-ease and dat-ease
"take one of these"

every time you sneeze
every time you squeeze
and push a little harder
the slave gets near the larder
but never close enough
theres a dog in every manger
it don't get any stranger
watch the signs there may be danger
from the Doktors of Despair
their Golden DIAGNOSIS
is bigger up the doses
a ring a ring a roses
atishoo....
atishoo....
the chemikal clowns
who run your town
keep dumbing you down
"keep your eyes on the ground"
"don't make a sound"
"nobody moves and no-one gets hurt"
"do I make myself clear?"
PUT YOUR HANDS IN THE AIR
"no-one moves, no-one gets hurt"
"no-one moves, no-one gets hurt"
"keep your feet in the dirt
"while we fleece your shirt"

"put your money in the bag
the one marked swag........!"
so you think your hard...?
well the barrel of this gun
is simply a loaded tongue
that holds you on a rung
of your own frustration
you must tune into this station

one love.......one vibration
here to heal the nation
get your "blag" outta your swag-bag

GET OOT......
have a good look
whats at the root?
a lie or the truth?
choose for yourself
theres a mountain of wealth
in your mental health
chemikal bombers of stealth
medicine off the shelf
........elektronik hair
intra-veinous armchairs
the Doktors of Despair
hold the set square
get inside us
redefine us
re-route our wiring
elektro-brain backfiring
pleasure from pain
nothing to gain
something to lose
you end up con-fused
your wiring's abused
by those who refuse
to admit they were wrong
keep singing their song
of mind over matter
the illusion must shatter
being healed by "mad-hatters"
it's no wonder we're bland
in this looking glass land
on foundations of sand
LOOK!.........
in the palm of your hand
the answer........ "overstand"
is at your command
make it real....make it live
you've so much to give
all your story is there to relive

but you've got to forgive
yourself for the pain
that you gave to your brain
you need love to remain
don't carry the stain
let your love reign
get in tune to your brain
the grey really matters
don't let your soul shatter
the grey really matters

22 twenty two 22 twenty2 Recurring

"think of a card!" said the roadside magician
who'd just hit town wearing the most
convoluted frown

A joiner in the earshot said "hold tight!....
I 'as one 'ere....and 'im don't wear a gown"
"....'es got bells upon 'im...so ye can see 'im
.......when ye can't see owt else"
So the magikman pulled a potion
........from the middle
..........of the bottom
..........of his top hat
to a round of bunny sandwiches
that represented the echo
...of a poem well red
or a rhyme well blue
designed to confuse you
with someone else
with a historikal bent
to learn what's meant
....by repent

"jack o' diamonds!" called the magikman
and the jack let out a whoop......
"I sure didnae see that comin'...
or hear you on the wind
....I caught no whiff of juniper
....nor taste of burning oak
across deserts I have flown
.....in search of the ghosts of forests
...that used to block out the sky
......forever coming eye to eye
.....with multinational vampire I
My sword is words.....and quick of silver
.....slieght of hand before your very eyes
I'll justly end the search..
from my vantage perch
I can see holoslaught on innernet
upon hurrycane
and earthy-quake
and poison snake
inside your head
where the crumbs of bred
don't pay pardon to the water
or the grass-snake
or his namesake
or his father
or his mother
or his brother
or any other
who care or bother...
what happens to the others"
So magikman and jack o' swords danced round and
round and out of sight and back again.... in
refreshing rain..

with a main-
line service
to the heady, deadly
rough and readily
available in a medley
of preconstructed sales-pitch melody

for voices trained in the art of deception

Jack sold one more bottle
then leant on the throttle
as Magik got his head down
with his wives in the back

"think of a card .." said jack with a grin
"Jack o' diamonds!" said a voice from within.

22 Recurring22 Recurring22 Recurring

so I venture out the University doors into the late evening sunshine
    I pull three shapes from last nights dream
    and manifest them in the here and now
    then the road melts away below my feet
    to be replaced with moorland gorse
     and the sound of men screaming and shouting
    deafens me as all around arrows flash through the air
    which is heavy with the stench of blood and despair
    entrails and anger and fear.....
        when a lame horse draws near
            and whispers in my ear.....
        "What you gonna do now, hairy man?"

"EASY" says I, as I click the heels of my red dancing slippers together
    and once more peace and calm reign
    and I am on top of Woodhouse moor
        but it seems to be getting dark too rapidly

and as I turn to see what is blocking out the sun
a charging stegasaurus on the run.........
Dropping and rolling sideways narrowly escaping death
I catch sight of the underside of its belly.......
there emblazoned the words   Disney Corporation
"Past Present and Future division"
blink my eyes in disbelief.......
and this bloke on Woodhouse Lane is saying
    "you all right mate?...........
        f**k me!....whats your name?.. MOSES?
"No" says I
"JUST ANOTHER BASKET CASE
  FLOATING DOWN THE RIVER..."
just another basket case floating down the river
'   just another bashet case floating down the river"

22 Recurring22 Recurring22 Recurring

I came off barbs very suddenly in Feltham
psychiatric borstal on a rubber mattress awash
with vomit.....drifting in and out of consciousness
hours and minutes melting like pizza cheese into
weeks and months.....
what year was that....?
what happened in the world that year......?
what was on the television that year.....?
who married who that year.....?
who was I that year........?
was I a junkie street kid........?
was I a menace to society......?
was I another statistic.......?
was I masochistic......?
or just sadistic.......
to myself...
to my memories...

of what the future might hold
childhood memories of apocalypse
in the here and now
Triple Trauma Typhoon
makes the child howl at the moon
running naked through the forest
feeling free, alive, at rest
barefoot pineneedles and moss
searching for something lost
scrambling over rocks and gorges
dark-eyes on, no need for torches
my "problem with society" disorder
manifest in nine year old border
BORDER..
      '   BORDER.....
"'BORDER.......
"back on the rubber matress....
WHERE AM I.......?
WHO AM I ?
am I in the past remembering the future?
or am I in the future imagining the past?
where is the present.....?
am I here now.....?
how will I know ?
where the future begins....

and the memory ends
neuro-message delay/send
body and soul no longer friends
existing purely to offend
head jammed down the S-bend
upside down feeling the rush
humiliation of the flush
that clears the works
in an underground cottage
searching for a vein
of pure gold
to keep me from the cold
flames of hell

no matter how I yell
the waiter never comes
aw' fuck...its the runs
they take it in turns
as my entrails churn
beneath an airware sole
another day in the hole
of the hollowed out tree
a faint smell of memory
rotting wood and mystery
childhood dreams of history
a wooden cave, an overcoat
a suit of armour made of oak
the court-jester who never jokes
trying hard not to choke
on the metallic liquid smoke
that's forced down my throat
and as I start to float
by the ferrymans boat
heading for that distant shore
he hits me with his bloody oar
just another slamming door

that wakes me on my rubber pallet
trying to kick another habit........

twenty two recurring

eleven ringing

someone singing

time .... runs back ...doors slam open and I tumble uphill
once more to that field in Wales ....Who's fingers are these?
Tapping these keys?
          I'm not sure..... the bones, the flesh
                    who is the person....? I get glimpses but no detail
No real substance, places, names, times..... just glimpses,
little flashes.....
Who is this person?
Is he some Bob Pirsig clone, Destroyed by order of a court?
*"Enforced by the transmission of high-voltage alternating current
through*
*The lobes of the brain. Approx 800mills of amperage at durations of
0.5 to 1.5 seconds applied on 28 consecutive occasions in a process
known technologically as"Annihilation ECT"*
          a whole person has been killed
          I have never met him
          I never will

          Though he must be here
          Still looking on........
          Watching what I'm doing with the remains of his body
          Little glimpses.....
                    Little flashes.....
                              Sparks.....
                                   Like the fleeting blue of a Kingfisher
          He's still in there......
                              Anarchic
                              Destructive
                              Uncontrolable
          He doesn't care much for this "new me"
          All bloody ladida and PC
          Who's fingers are these?
          Tapping these keys
          He wants me to be outrageous
          I must hold it together
          He wants me to kill this personality
          And get another......

" Better shock next time"
He repeats endlessly as if the phrase holds some humour
  Who's fingers are these?

I MET A MAN........
I met a man who could recite all twenty three thousand
lines of the "Romance of the Rose" but could not count to five.
  '

I met a man who could recite pi to one thousand decimal points
but could not find a rhyme for love nor money

I met a man who laughed at every thing that wasn't funny
I met another who cried for ever because he was so happy
and another who laughed at his pain
and one who lost all he'd gained

I met a man who sailed the ocean blue
in search of pastures blue
He told me he was searching for the "beginning of the end"
so I sold him a postcard and he nailed it to the mast
then I stepped into his past
and went to meet his King
who was laying on the ground
whilst his bodyguards around
put the boot into him
like L.A. droogs with Rodney King
history just sings
endlessly repeating itself
forever shedding it's skin
cleansing the kin
thinning and culling
and making a date with SIN......
       ....ACTIC FOLLY

I met a woman who remembered
what life was like before Adam

I met a woman whose hair scattered rainbows everywhere
as she danced in the moonlight

I met a woman who was me and she set me free

I met a man who could measure words to the nth degree
he taught me heresy
and how to pray
and how to give it all away
then he asked me to pay
for HIS fathers crimes
 so I said "NO WAY"
and later that day
he tied me to the wheel
but I refused to feel
and I swore to heal
the wounds of my inquisitor

Well I met a man who said "I khan
unite all the nomads on the land"
he said "I'll lay it all to waste
and the rivers shall taste
worse than bodily waste"
so I went to see my Mother
to ask if there was any other
                    WAY
to gain an extra day?
as the climate starts to sway
She said "have your say....
          .....then be on your way"

Well I met a man and he taught me how to surf
on the crust of molten magma
and I met a little boy
who taught me the joy
of playing in inner space

Well I met a man from the future
travelling back in time

who said "excuse me Mr. RHYME?"
   "...but I've come from a time
where wrappers are disposable
parts of a product"

"careful how you juggle
your verbs and your vowels
may get you into trouble"
so I burst his bubble
with a "sword" that I drew
from my grandmothers sock
which came as a shock
to the "thought police"
who were waiting in the street
with their "crosswords" COCKED
and their 'double entendres " primed
looking for some crime
of the cerebral kind
but I met this woman
who said " climb into my body and come with me
                    to the Ancestors' tree
so I climbed aboard and I clung on tight
as her body rose to the highest height
and she showed me what might
or might not come to pass
then she lowered me down
by the hem of her gown
called me her "linguistic clown"
which made me frown
as I looked all around
to see where she'd gone

and a voice from the past said
"look inside your head
she is not dead
haven't you read
a word that you've said?"

I met a woman who scattered rainbows from her hair
I met a woman who was me and she set me free

So who are you? Says the echo in my head...."who are
you?.. folk need to know which way the wind blows ?"
...let me introduce myself
I'm known by many names...
        Some of them unprintable
and some of them just too strange?

I've been called jesus, moses, Manson
Crusty Hippy Scum!
Dirty pagan bastard
Disgusting scrounging noun

So ...let me introduce myself
I'm known by many names...
        Some of them unprintable
and some of them just too strange?

Some call me a chastifier
even Brimstone and Fire
but I'm not a chatty fire
I'm no righteous liar
I'm a loose wire
I'm a toaster
I'm not a boaster (but)
I built Nelson's Column
I built the Coliseum
I burn down museum
I burn down deisel engine
I cool down fire engine
I rough up petrol head
I cough up Red Red Red

I cough cough car fume
I cough cough per fume
I less less consume
I more more confuse
As I see child get a buse
I more more confuse
as the poor get fleeced by quick dealers
and the sick get access to less Healers
and the healers run to heal the wealthy
and redesign the breasts of the healthy
So..I just have to say
I'm just a toaster
a talking toaster
Would you like it well done?
shall I singe it wi' ma tung?
Aye yi herd me right
hiv yi goat a light?
did somewan mention "fire next time"
av goat sum wurk to do
an it isnae mine....
My Mother is crying
I've come from her lungs
To speak for my children
To speak for my Ancestors
To work for my Mother
Who gave birth to your Kings
Who in turn stole your birthright
Who sold your children into slavery
Who frighten your Elders into prison
Who separate the Families
Who separate the Tribes
Who separate the vibes
Who separate the races
Who separate the species
Who separate the all

Who operate for none
Who benefit for some
Who laugh up their sleeve
Who invent up disease
Who plan how to kill
and sell you a thrill
and build a tread-mill
and a carrot and stick
to prove to your master
that you really are sick
get a note from your doktor
to exempt you the next bit

better get a fireproof suit
Walk in the desert and search for a root
My people are waiting…..
while you count your loot
My people are waiting….
for you to leave the Garden
My people are waiting….
to see what you leave
My people are waiting
to count the damage done
My people are ready..
just leave when you done
My people are forgiving
and shall always be
forever healing the damage that you do
Though you couldn't understand us
You judged us and you burnt us
You ethnically cleansed us
You passed acts of god to kill us
You persecuted my sister
You religious twister
You have twisted your minds

Against all Womankind
You exalt her into bondage
and sell her brother the keys
so she can be sold by commodity brokers
and decisions about her child bearing rights
are made by men in wigs

So … I just haffi say
I a toasta
a talking toaster
in a strange land
Where baby girls are less valued
than their sterile brothers
Where shaving the body is desirable
Where cutting dogs tails is fashionable
Where plants can be criminal
Where altered states are not spiritual
Where abuse is habitual
the people turn gullible
and get re-educated by cathode ray nipple
and internet mice
Whilst taking a slice
from everyone's pie
And selling the Sky
to people who believe
that it can be "owned"
where the air is policed
and water is metered
and profits are made
from selling the rain
that began its cycle
in the consumers bladder
and fell from the sky
that smells like a sty

and enters your lungs
and touches everyone

even the King in his castle
in the thin mountain air
can see fires in the forest
and the smoke stings his eyes
as down in the valley
the riot-cops scream
and vagrants dream
of lives that are better
but not by much
as strangers drop coins
that they use as a crutch
to maintain their importance
of being no-one important
to the rules of the game
by paying the balance
then Justice is Served
in the clink of metal tokens
that fall into a Hat
at a place called Redemption
in a land called accusation
of constant reminders to toe the line
So remember, give willingly, but not too much
if the beggar leaves then you'll have his pitch
and a chance to get rich
on wisdom and advice
and.."do you know what I think?"
        "you'll spend it on drink..!"
        "you'll spend it on drugs!"
"honest I won't mister...
    I'll spend it on waste
        I'll get a piece of metal

and dig a hole in my Mothers face
Big enough to swallow
    all the metal discs
     that you toss into my hat"

So you see my scam at last
I simply throw them back
I toss them in the ocean
I throw them to the breeze
I burn your paper promises
I set the carbon free
the carbon that is all of us
the root of every tree
the heart of every seed
the light in every leaf
the light that I am harvesting
the seed that I am storing
getting ready for the fall…
Of your own preconceptions
Of how its meant to be
Of how its going to be
Of how its always been
Of the reality of Nature
Of the perception of reality
of a dog in every manger
and a wolf dressed as a lamb
of drugged controlled children
in schools of hypocrisy
Where they learn how to want
and they learn to compete
and go through the maze
and get a pat on the head
and wake up Dead
in the middle of a Mall
having heard nothing at all

except a bit of a rant
from a beggar itinerant
just a man near the edge
living on veg
with a smile on his lips
and love in his heart
and a Dog at his feet
just working the street
about his belief…
that perception is reality